Worms Eat Our Garbage

Katie Sharp

Illustrated by Kathy Mitchell

Rigby

Our class wanted to learn about worms.
"Worms eat garbage," said Mr. Roberts.
"I will show you.
After lunch bring me some food."

3

After lunch Mr. Roberts said,
"We are going to make a home
for our worms."
First he put small holes
in the bottom of a pail.

Then he put newspaper and dead leaves into the pail.
Finally he put in some dirt and water.

newspaper

leaves

dirt

water

Mr. Roberts pulled some worms
out of a bag.
The worms wiggled in his hand.
"Yuck!" the class shouted together.

Everyone put food into the pail.

Pierre put in a banana peel.

Katie put in carrot sticks.

Manuel put in part of his bread.

"Our worms will eat the garbage and the food," said Mr. Roberts.

We put the pail in a dark closet.
We hoped that Mr. Roberts was right.

After two days, we took the pail
out of the closet.
All of the garbage and food was gone!
Mr. Roberts was right.
"How did the worms eat everything?"
asked Pierre.

"Worms like to dig," said Mr. Roberts.
"They dig and eat dirt, dead leaves, and food."

14

"The worms make new dirt
that helps plants grow," said Mr. Roberts.

"Worms really do eat garbage," said Katie.

"Can we give them more?" asked Pierre.

"Yes," said Mr. Roberts. "These worms
will eat all the garbage and food
they can get!"